THE HAN

for my Mother and Father

Frances Sackett
THE HAND GLASS

seren

seren
is the book imprint of
Poetry Wales Press Ltd.
First Floor, 2 Wyndham Street
Bridgend, Wales, CF31 1EF

© Frances Sackett, 1996

Cataloguing In Publication Data for this book
is available from the British Library

ISBN: 1-85411-167-1

*The publisher acknowledges the financial assistance of the
Arts Council of Wales*

Cover painting:
'Vanity', 1907 oil on canvas, by Frank Cadogan Cowper
by permission of the Royal Academy of Art

Printed by
Creative Print & Design Wales
Ebbw Vale

Contents

oðþæt wordes ord
brēost-hord þurhbræc
Beowulf (lines 2792-2793)

Until the word's point
broke through the breast-hoard
Beowulf (lines 2792-2793)

We must be still and still moving
Into another intensity.
T.S. Eliot, *Four Quartets*

Aurora

It was a place of red dawns —
A gasp from the earth's forge.
Vermilion and crimson and coral were in it

Winter was in it somewhere —
The demons of winter —
Hooded travellers from the Pole's edge.

There were no clefts in it,
Except once, a white jet peeled a strip from it.

Resurrection was in it
Yet Doomsday was in it too.

There was music in it —
The sound of dispersing notes
Floating away to edges of air.

There was amazement in it;
It amazed itself profoundly.

        In the silence,
Before speech-bearers woke,
It came up — red.

Turning Point

There is no land between Cape Wrath and the North Pole,
The eagle homes in against the die-hard sun,
Solos in technicolour,
Inbreathes air from the ice-caps,
Planes to pockets of snow.

It was here the longships turned south,
Searching for unbitten land, women, plunder.
Curlews scream above Am Buachaille,
Are dazzled by their own confusions
In the mountain pools.

Vanity

After a painting by F.C. Cowper, 1877-1958

The painter wanted embellishments,
What else could I do but dream and admire?
The props had never been so interesting,
Turning my cheeks to fire, filling the hand-glass
With a multitude of flashes, that flew like
Jolted planets, across the scanty sky of cloth
Set up behind.

       Such a change from angel-white —
The sultry taffeta, brocade in chains
Like gilded snakes that swarmed my arms,
My hands so formally arranged
To show the rings and touch the pearls
That wound their way around my neck,
Then trailed and looped against
The silken chair.

       And so he calls me 'Vanity'
And makes me feel the guilt of all
His observation. I only bared my shoulders
Once before, and that was when
A boy I loved said beauty lay
In what was unadorned.

Girl at the Piano

The child is deep in her music,
Forgotten her mother and father

Who sit in the sepia room,
The woman engrossed with her songbirds
Stuffed in their flightless dome,

Her husband glazing his eyes
With pipe smoke;

Feeling the back of the chair
Push deeper into his spine.

In the mirror above
Someone receives a bouquet,
Adulation,
Filling her arms
With its weight.

Franz Schubert

After the aquatint by Georg Eisler

Is it possible — to sit like that
And dream your pieces straight on to the keys?

The light that hits your glasses makes you
Blindman, poet, scribe, who only need

A little space in which to work. But space
Which takes a million images on board.

The images you seek — will they transcribe to
Notes, then chords, then bars?

Your head is glowing with the resonance —
You only need to take the journey now

To make your brain give out its messages
That move to muscles, down to fingers

And make them play
And play the room away.

Beyond the Door

She was familiar with the sound of the key —
A dull clunk outside the door.
Each time the walls moved in like wardens
Until the window breathed them out again.

She knew if she cried hard it would mean
Bruises which spread like dull clouds
Across her pink skin;
— That a quiet persistent whine
Sometimes brought food skidding across the floor.

Lying on her blanket she watched a moving light
Trace out a fluttering pattern on the wall.
Her tiny fingers smoothed the shapes
Like sable brushes painting blossom trees.

When broken sounds from outside drifted to her room
She wanted to trap them like imagination's toys;
To keep the outside in at all costs.
But like the rhythmic music of rain
They would drift away again.

One night through the uncurtained window she saw
                                a single star,
Its brilliant light cracked across the pane.
Then through the cracks the star came in,
She took it with her
                Beyond the door
                        That never locked again.

The Collector

Bartok was passionate about the songs.
While boundaries moved, places changed names,
He searched for Hungary's essence;
Divined for ancient tunes.

He was the alchemist,
His music both primitive and new;
Matched to something his soul had known
Was there, before he heard it.

His inner voice would listen
While a hawk soared and soared
Across the sallow sky
To dip and rise against the snow-capped peaks.

He heard vibrations when the wind
Soughed in the unbowing pines,
A distant tuning up through fir cones
That mimicked stark, barbaric rhythms.

Sometimes the sombre vastness of the plains
Would take him to the edge of man's existence:
The earth throbbing beneath his feet,
Grasses whistling dissonant notes.

A squall of night sounds haunted him,
The eagle shadowing the moon,
Yet still he kept his sight and thirst
Replenished at the natural spring.

The land's memories, beaten out in dance,
He dotted across staves —
Quintessential marks on boundaries,
Moving, unremitting.

A Dream of Birds

'I dreamt of birds,' she said,
Still in the grip of the tarantula's web.
We'd brought her from Gatwick,
Through English borders,
Stopped in a Cotswold village.

She spoke of home in the East,
Reminded us of ghostly forests
Where lichen spread like warts,
'And now strange mushrooms grow'
She said, 'so huge, mysterious.'

'I had a dream...'
We'd caught her watching from the car
The languid flight of birds,
The pastel sky that smoothed to chocolate soil,
The way the trees were flighty, individual.

And then her shock —
Stock still she stood
As fruit cascaded from a shop-front
In garish green and orange,
Promiscuous row on row.

Then flowing with the fruit
Her tears, releasing strand
By strand the weakening web.
Her voice now lifting, soaring,
'I dreamt of birds,' she said.

Christening the World

You're right, I must rename love;
It's a word we have all worn through.
If you like, I'll christen the world
And all its words for you.
　　　　　　　　　— 'No Title' (*Poems 1955-1959*)
　　　　　　　　　　　Pasternak

I am reading you and reading you
Pasternak. But not in your native tongue,
Although my eyes keep shifting to the left
Where Russian characters are dressing
Each left page so gallantly.

Neither is it the scrawl that Olga
Waited desperately to see in prison —
That made her dream of cranes and freedom.
But something of the passion moves
Between the words, organic by translation.

What you say to me is somehow
In neither of the languages
But somewhere outside syllable and grammar —
A place that geography can not pinpoint.

Too strange how your words keep
Loading me and loading me
Yet take me away
So often from the page.

Olga Ivinskaya was Pasternak's mistress who was imprisoned
because of her association with him.

Angle of Vision

Friedrich knew Dresden.
He knew it as an artist would —
Its colour, curves and atmosphere:
The city he called 'German Florence'.

He painted *Woman at the Window,*
Breathing in the sounds and smells
That drifted from the Elbe —
Domestic scenes that showed a gentle
Solidness exuding from the wood.

But Friedrich also looked with telescopic lens —
Down a gallery of visions,
And from a widening darkness
Brought to light, *The Large Enclosure* —

A vast, malleable arena,
Where the livid horizon tilts flat ground,
Mud-flats seethe like a whirlpool,
A coil of trees is smoke unfurling.
And the colours are colours of
Ash, sulphur and cindered skin.

And in another painting —
Man looking down on his
Own foggy landscape.

Prinsengracht 263 — Amsterdam

if I look up into the heavens...
— The Diary of Anne Frank, 15 July 1944.

You could just make it out —
The Westerkerk tower —
Through that arched window
In Peter's attic.

Now the large annexe windows
Are thrown wide,
Bells ring from the tower,
Pigeons coo in the back garden,
Buds break out on the old trees,
A cat yawns on a low rooftop.

We pay our toll —
Move in a long snake
Through the rooms,
English rubbing shoulders with Dutch,
German, Japanese, American.
The air, a slow mingling of garlic,
Spices and perfumes.
We read in our optional languages.

A mirror reflects the loft —
Exactly as I imagined it.

I would like to tell you, Anne,
That the house still stands tall —
Looks down at itself in the canal
And shivers a little at its memories;
As though by reflecting its good side
It could always trust in humanity
Having perfect manners
Like the people now
Passing through.

At Lidice

At Lidice there are no loud echoes —
The flame that blew through windows
Like curtains is phoenix ash
Deep in the land.
White convolvulus is tying the grasses
Together like the twining of arms
When wives clung to husbands,
Children to their mothers.
A stone frieze depicts their story.

On a slope of land
That catches the morning sun
The children in bronze stand —
Stare straight ahead.
One sucks his thumb,
One scratches his wrist —
His hands almost a prayer.
Young girls fold arms
To younger siblings.
A boy nearly grown hides
At the back of the group, his foot
Turned at an angle for running,
His eyes mature.

Convolvulus traces the boundary
Of old Lidice —
Will not leave this land alone.

Lidice was the small Czech village razed to the ground by the Nazis in June 1942, as retribution for the mortal wounding of Reinhard Heydrich.

No Blossoms in Dubrovnik

Spring, 1993

Turn in the road —
The easy-chair of England,
Trees doing what they always do
This time of year —
The oak, the beech,
Producing buds that just a week ago
Were raindrops on the bough.

And Spring will rage around us now,
Each day encroaching nearer
On our windows,
And England sits back easy
In its chair to watch
The flagrant dissolution
Of a season with its cities
Brought through the glass
Of smaller windows
Right inside the rooms;

A season blasted back to earth
Where ashes of a culture
Already fill the crevices —
Blow in no direction
Except where winds will take them;
As easily toss refuse
As any refugee.

This year —
No blossoms in Dubrovnik.

Impromptu Display

When it rains in Split
The skaters come out.
Water on the statues
Water on their lips;
They join up hands
And skate across the square.

The sudden thunder,
Then the rain
Darkens marble cobbles
Makes them sleek as slugs;
Cobalt under water
Pitted by the rain.

Tourists under awnings
Darken wind-blown lace —
Watch the rain-splashed skaters
Water on their lips
Skating over cobbles
When it rains in Split.

River Music

My childhood was spent near rivers;
Music running through my veins,
Either singing, almost imperceptibly, in deep water,
Or ringing in the shallows over wide, flat stones.

I would listen to the story of rivers,
(Just as Nureyev watched trains, dreamed
Of other lands, and dancing through them).
The river was traveller and escapee —

Unbridled in its urge to carve a way.
Its precincts held sacred things:
The kingfisher, in startling outward flight,
As though the valley flashed an open eye

And in an instant slept again,
The Druid circle, with its damp intensity —
An ancient ring of whisperings;
A Celtic cranium for eternity.

A river tried to claim me once —
It rocked me deep with cradle hymns,
Then gave me back to light and air and birdsong.
I often question this.

Pinch Yourself

Sometimes when turning the last bend home,
The car swimming the curve like an angel,
Laburnum scenting the air
In the fluid-dark of the street,
You feel that you're not really living
But play-acting life in a film,
Running — re-running —
Monotony even in death.

Reminds you of going to your birthplace,
Searching the bends in the river,
Looking for the dark, deep pool —
Unable to find it —
The place insisting in echoes
You drowned there — drowned there.

The Poet Reading

Water, in a stemmed goblet
Curves the reflected notice-board
To its own contours.
Papers become camellias
In this watery medium.
I hear his mobile mouth
Articulate a flow of words
But analyse with painter's eye
The light, the shade, the convolutions.
The brilliant plane of light
Where water meets the air
Could float me like Ophelia —
And native to the element
Transpose me to his world.
I keep my gaze within
The globe — the form retaining
Endless permutations.
He reads his journey through
And then takes water,
Quenching his fluency;
Drunk in his world
Of paper, poetry, sparkle,
Refracted reality.

Change of Weather at Conwy

Chimney-smoke curling from slate roofs
Then blowing out seaward like a squall.
Sky lightening momentarily — magnolia-petalled,
Shifting a sifting of cloud against castle parapets
(A feather-light caress as flesh warms on flesh)
And pouring a prism of yellow
Laser-angled at Deganwy.
(Caught in the glow and melting within sunlit rooms.)

Gulls standing sentinel, spanning
Turret, quay and quiff of a wave,
(From stronghold to height in rhythm with the sea)
Their cries echoing history through dank castle walls
Of battles fought in fervour — now extinguished.
(Enmeshed, entangled, abandoned in sheer exhaustion
Like nets along the quay.)

Another Kind of Skin

You had a skirt with flounces;
Scenes from *My Fair Lady*,
That gathered to your slim waist,
Laid youth on your child-bearing frame.

Your domestic routines were like
Miniature seasons: Mondays
Washing, Tuesdays ironing,
Wednesdays — the big bake.

One summer day you came
Out to the garden. Look, you said,
And spread before us
Manicured nails, brightly painted red.

Your skirt with its pictures
Blew in the breeze,
You displayed your fingers
As though your behaviour was risky —

A sudden unveiling of woman —
Not for the likes of a mother
With three growing children.

Arthritic

I used to watch you
Slip off wax, opaque
And white, like gloves,

Believing that your knuckles'
Pain would soften into ripples,
Harden, peel away.

Then surgeons chipped the chalk,
Put pins in place
And gave your thumbs agility.

In shops your palm became a hole
That sometimes caught the change,
Depending if the aims were slick.

As science follows surgery
The race is never won,
And doctors climb the ladder

Disc by disc, to view
Through x-ray's ghostly plate
The structural degeneration.

And I have seen you climb
The stairs on hands and knees
And tell me that you should not

Place your knuckles so —
Though having no facility
To spread them flat

You fist up their atrocities
And steer your insect crawl.

The Walled Orchard

The walled orchard tingles
With the remnants of rain
Wind-rushed in the treetops.
Tiny carmine apples dangle
Beads of rain like teats.
Carnations circle a stone
Like an exposed eye ball —
A pool of water in its cave-hole
Muddy and mossed,
Deep as an iris.
One tree with a flick of blossom —
A tiny pink bud with wings.
Snap-dragons rooted through mortar
Like foot-holds,
Stencilling the old, pink brick.
Now the rank stink of vegetation
Pours from the earth,
Fuchsias drip red-painted fingernails
Over the bench,
Rain begins again
Swarming in the treetops.

Return Fair Eve

How is it
That this displaced rib,
Now given flesh and shape
And earthy countenance,
Still feels related —
Yet will not comfortably fit again
Without encroaching on my heart?

Her sinewy form
Now gliding through the orchard
And teasing apples from the
Wayward, knotted branches,
Will maybe shun perfection there —
Recall instead the delicate flowering,
The soft-blown blossom —
Resembling flesh on bone.

A Quality of Loss

You turn it over and over in your hand,
Not wanting to finger its feathers
Of flight with your skin, but with tissue.

So beautiful, you say. *Only death,*
Only natural. The nuthatch lies soft
In its greys, its pigments suffused
With the morning — the palest of beams
Spreading wide the dark wing.

Is it freedom from something, and natural,
So much flight, so much liberty,
Still, in the palm of your hand?

Unfinished

Only an illusion —
As I look to the tip of the spire
And against the scudding clouds
The whole of Salisbury's steeple
Seems set to tip and fall.

The frisson is daunting —
More so than knowing
Its masons were resolved
To leave their work unfinished
For others to complete.

At Stonehenge,
A temple positive,
Clamped to the plain
Where jackdaws nest
And home within its labyrinths.

The hengemen always knew
That as they hefted forth each stone
The work would finish them
Before they saw an end.

The way we speed at life
Makes little difference now,
Although we shape illusions
That life will write a coda
When all our dreams are realised.

So I regret I never knew
What promises you had for yours
My father — dying young
And I too young to ask;

My mother never knowing
Or memory eroded —
Or else, bereft of her illusions,
Forgetting we erect them.

I close my eyes
And when I open them again
The sky is blue with scudding clouds
And falling rapidly I see
A spire of white — pure poetry.

Tulips

Everyone is alone on the heart of the earth
pierced by a ray of sun:
and suddenly it's evening.
— Salvatore Quasimodo

Why does he bring me tulips now?
  Flames of sunset drop
    From the ramrod stems
      Shine like reflections on a slate sea.

I am possessed by their progress:
  One whole flower yowls
  Its mouth agape with gold-dust.
  Hung over, another bloom
  Gleams like china
  Deceiving me —
     Oh the deception —
  Of the death to come
  In slow drops
  Of demon's rain
  Until green profusion
  Is alone
  And starkly voiceless.
And suddenly it's evening.

The Sun Declining

I watch you and you seem
To swell
Between the angle of the oak's
Huge thrusting branches.

You fade —
And all that clarity —
A lucid Japanese silk-print

Turns into mist
And smoky coral —
Slips down between
The satin sheets
Of April's evening.

Don't go —
I want to see a permanence
Beyond the ancient trees
And dancing saplings.

You go —
Before I write your epitaph
This poem on the page.

The Tempter or the Tempted

Move now, before I take
Too much from your eyes,
Before your hand — that wants to —
Strays to my hair
Or touches again
The nearest exposure of skin.

Hold back your trespassing foot,
Do not begin again
The sentence that you started,
Lost in trepidation;
Fallen now in thought.

Move now,
Before this language that we play
Turns into words.

Henry Moore

This was no laying on of hands,
But he saw at once
The sky's potential
Pouring through the stone.

Beyond reclining figures of the shelters
Where lines of bodies spread like bones,
There was a pantheistic world
Drowning under Yorkshire skies —
A form the slag heaps printed
Through the mists of dawn.

He knew the light would alter
Every shape he cast —
Gave up his concrete forms to mystic space.

His naked bronzes warming in the sun
Record a pagan contact;
Stinging heat on nipples,
Candid breeze that riffles
Into ravines — down the alley
Of the spine.

We never feel the elements so close;
The landscape in us, round us, through us.

Our hands are aching — empty.
We lay them on the bronze.

One Little Room

I have a tan all year.
— Pride myself on it.
Body beautiful and no tide marks.

It's relaxing after a day at work
To slip between the perspex sheets,
Naked and sweating, and let your mind go blank.

I worship the bedroom carpet
That my god reclines on.
No packing and waiting at airports for me.

The golden lands can stay unseen.
As far as I'm concerned
My body is my golden land.

When I switch on at night
The sun fills my room —
Blue to every corner.

The Degas 'Dancing Girl of Fourteen Years'

Protected by glass
Eyes half closed,
The 'Dancing Girl of Fourteen Years'
Draws her audience.

The proud head,
Body still in chrysalis,
And somehow, the clenched illusion
Transient in the bronze glow.

She turns you, turns you —
Until you feel the hands of Degas
Reworking in the air
She seems to breathe.

Did she ever dance?
Did the butterfly emerge to mock
The humble background and sweep
Gazelle-like in the lamplit Opera glow?

Inside that trance she's dancing now,
On and on in a mesmeric beat of pirouettes
Until dust and light fuse —
Truth and illusion fuse.

Préparation

In the name of the dance
In the name of that bondage
My feet turn out and round like cogs.

Pavlova, Markova, Fonteyn.

The room is shuttered,
Light filtered,
The barre is constant — punishing,
My knee is lifted, hip turned out
And round, pulled round.

The sweat is trickling,
The heat obscuring
Beams that trace the wooden floor.
I beat to music
Music beats me,
Turn out my foot, my foot turns out.

My arms are gentle,
Gentling air
To attitude before my eyes.
The dream is constant —
In the shadows,

Markova, Pavlova, Fonteyn.

The floor is rising,
Its sinews stretching,
My fingers make their bird-like shapes.
The shadows claim me
One more victim,
My feet turn out, turn out.

I Heard My Name

Van Gogh, 1987

The gavel thump recalled a shot
Resounding through a sea of corn,
The 'Sunflowers' sold for such a price —
Their latent power so overdue —
They seared my heart when first I saw
Their cadmium tones outstare the sun;
'O Theo, send me fifty francs, I have
No canvases or paint.'

The mistral force is in me now
It swarms my head with crows and dust
Frenzied brush strokes sweep me on
To visions coursing for release;
The waving corn now feels my ebb,
In far Provence the mistral whines
And casts the seeds of sunflowers wide.
I cannot say goodbye in words
Provence will sign my last still-life.

Mary in the Galilee Chapel — Durham Cathedral

After Polish sculptor Josef Pyrz

In the Galilee chapel
Mary faces the window;
Carved in golden wood
Her rib cage ranged like wings.

How did the sculptor begin
To feel for that look on her face?
Quite rightly he gives us an angel
In woman-bone raiment.

But how transcend her confusion
When she cast about in her mind
For the manner of salutation
That Gabriel confronted her with?

Highly favoured of women —
Is this what she wanted to be?
So humbling to be blessed,
But to learn humble!

Finding a balance, after such
Sensitive shaping of grain,
Must be like the stillness
Returning

After peering at fathoms of drop
Down flashes of air
To the Wear, then turning
Back from the window
To Mary's long glance.

Newly Delivered Mother

You will learn it very slowly —
The craft of motherhood.
No sage has taught you anything
That comes as new as this.
The baby swathed in cloth beside you,
Cocooned in light, is god-like;
Still sailing from its amniotic berth.
And by the way you lift
Your hand to touch —
But not quite touch,
And by the way
The fragile air between you
Whispers its seduction,
The world is love — all love.

The Naming

So simple, the way grey light
Seeps through slits of darkness
Making milky contours of the land.
Offering, yet holding back as yet
Its shift to blanket-light,
A long, slow flow of
Giving out its gifts,
A coolness drawn on, bathed in, drunk in,
A silent lesioning of clouds
To show their pap of peachy fruits
Fletching all the east.
So simple, after holding you through this,
To name you Dawn.

Letter to Rodin from Gwen John

Such a room I have taken now —
In the rue Cherche-Midi.
It is the prettiest ever.
I am painting a corner of it:
My narrow pine table under
The window, a jar of primroses,
The wicker chair to the side of it.
I wake to sunlight streaming
Through the muslin curtain.

I am a blue flower growing
High in the Alps — enduring your absence.
No, I am a waif, a vagabond
Without you. *Cher ami* come home soon.
I try to put a morsel of my heart
To one side in order to paint.
Art is a little beating heart, you say.
I believe you. But now my heart
Is elsewhere and my soul demands
To hear your step on the stair.

At this distance I fear
The leap of our flesh
Will cool
Our kisses turn to stone.

Driving Home from the Opera

The car smoothly curving in unison
With white lines and zig-zag bends;
Carmen's flight to the mountains
Would have been better staged in this landscape;
The sky dazzled with stars,
Bizet's music echoing still in these hills.
I fix my eyes on Venus
Her magnetic brilliance pulling
Like that other pull
Within the car.

I will you to stop the car,
Enclose me in your arms,
Knowing it would not happen;
Too many years and habits
Traverse this warm, close distance
And your eyes only for the road
Ignore my telepathic call.

After the Anaesthetic

I knew your eyes were blue,
I'd always thought them grey-blue.

If you were asked to name the hue
Of mine, you might or might not know.

After the operation, I couldn't wait
To see you back in the world

We both inhabit; returned from somewhere
I had never been.

As I entered your room, messages moved like
Radar. You wanted touch to be

Your first sensation. With an effort drawn
From the depths, like shoots that surface earth,

Your fingers reached for mine. Above
The oxygen mask, your eyes for seconds woke.

The blue was cornflower, harebell, bluebell.
Can anaesthetic do that?

Corn Dolly

Once, I took you from your hook,
Prepared to throw you out —
You'd gathered dust for years
And any fertile properties you had
Were icons I could do without.
But something stopped me —
I wondered about the hands
That had twisted an intricate
Barley-sugar circle
And placed it on the phallic stem;
I wondered at the sheen that
Held the sun's flame
Within the corn's silk —
The seeds that scattered from the tassel,
That sounded all the rustling
Bells of cornfields as you walked through them,
Mouth-high to their aroma,
Feeling the sharp stems
Tack at your pubescent legs —
Knowing that in a few weeks
They would be gathered to stooks
And stride the fields like
Wigwams under moonlight.
I shook you loose of your dust
And heard the wind leap
Across fields,
Skim through the furrows,
Holla a song of high summer.

Siesta

This noon-stillness oozes from high walls,
Drifts its heat through narrow streets,
Makes limp the leaves of plants in pots
And sweats the vines around the doors
Like girls who flag from chores, collapse
In chairs or hammocks and finger hair
From brows in languid gestures.
It lingers in the square where empty
Tables bake the rings from coffee cups
And on the sides of steps,
Where melon rinds put out for skinny cats
Drink up their own pink flesh,
And wasps around the shops where fruit
Has dripped its sweet oasis in the dust
Can only raise a lazy buzz occasionally —
Until the sea wind lifts it to the hilltop
And from the bell-tower doves free-fall
Like snow above hibiscus trees.

Gathering Wood

She's walking towards a September smoulder in the sky,
Gathering wood for her last winter.
Her old coat dips one side from where she pulls it closer;
A kite shape, ready to be lifted by the wind.
The air is timber-cool and wood-smoke warm,
The sky in ashen softness makes another country.
She would step into it if she could,
Let go her old entanglements.
She places acorn branches, rowan twigs,
Amongst the fallen dead wood —
A sack so full of treasures they ignite
The dark and dusty cloth.
A glowing fire is wrapping round her edges,
The backs of leaves quicksilvering the night;
She can hear already the hum of fire in wood —
Already see a stepping off.

Le Cygne

After Mallarmé

Virginal, living and beautiful day,
Break with wild wing
This frozen, alien lake where ice hides
A prism of phantom shadows.

A swan, caught between air and water,
Remembers his hopeless struggle for release
When sterile winter was radiant and he
Immobile to sing his country's song.

His neck moves in tragic, white agony
Unable to deny the pristine air
Unable to break from his glass snare.

Futile to think of freedom —
His phantom brilliance is part
Of the cold dream of exile.

Ice

They have fired their houses,
Now they want ice.
They take the mountain road,
Toil the path in a dark cord
Following their leader — tribal again.
All questions have left them;
Questions require answers
And answers are grit
That pierce their feet
Clog between their toes —
May prevent their exodus.
In the distance — on the topmost
Mountains their eyes light on
White. They will drag the ones
That fall. Hitch them under their arms.
In a few hours they will reach it —
That thing they dream of.
Then they will kneel
To view their changed reflections.
Ice — it numbs their fingers —
Their lips —
The only pure thing left.

The Journey

in memory of Susannah Howell

The day kept everything under wraps:
The trees were armoured in their ice,
White fields bristled, long grasses
Were swords of glass at the road's edge,
Not a tear of ice fell to indent
The sealed earth.

In the church her name sang —
Susannah, Susannah —
Just as she had cracked hearts
With her rendering of *Bread of Heaven.*

She was back in her valleys now.
This land — this crematorium —
Was static — wearing white.
Only the breath of the bereaved
Softened out in the air,
Lifted to distance,
Circled the trees in wreaths.

Wintirfyllith

*Wintirfyllith is Anglo-Saxon for when the
first full moon of winter could be seen.*

i.

The clouds furled with their weight of snow.
The trees flamed with the last of their tinder.
Shadows of trunks made huge candelabra
On the linen of uncrossed land.

Inked to the distance, the dark mountain
Gave little comfort. I lie here,
It seemed to say, at my own level —
And always your forest grows in my shadow.

ii.

The land is full of winter
Carved out in runes.
Rock flames with the tree —
Sword of light —
Star from the stone.

Twilight slips down the sky,
River fruits in the moon,
Woman hands man fire,
Stone is flesh in the star.

Winter Solstice Poems

i.

Painting for therapy — and love,
She chooses Van Gogh to copy,
Loads her brush with blues
And paints his 'Starry Night'.

She whirls between the stars,
She helter-skelters ridges;
Scales the cypress' summit,
Capsizes in the sky.

ii.

I tell her of our journey
Through frozen Shropshire air —
How we braked hard
To avoid the imbecile driver,

How our hearts reared
To stallion stance,
Then beat
Refrain on refrain of existence.

After weeks of dark tunnels
She talks of the shortest day —
How light will now lengthen
Its reach — seep out the grey hours,

Freshen the air of burnt sacrifice.
I look at the view to the west —
Soft-bleed through a bandage of sky —
But agree that things change,

Though unable to close out the dusk,
Or connect with a tone of summer.

iii.

Is there a safe harbour inside the self?
Is it summer imagined
From the depth of winter solstice,

Summer with its flags of light
Like the cumulus of sails
Racing to the quayside,

The imagined green arbour
That birds inhabit
In their fragrant treetops,

An imagined love
That pours into every corpuscle
Of hair and skin,

Keeping its plenitude,
Like mountain lakes
Fed with the melting of snows?

Or can the battlement of the body
Only take so many reinforcements;
Desert to a hillside,

Sit with impunity,
And watch its rough tides
Break on the harbour wall?

Rite of Spring

All winter she wore her clothes skin-tight,
A winding sheet of frost-shot leaves,
Her limbs a lattice-lace of ice.
She stood within the open wood,
Her roots in touch with earth's dark crypt;
Drew down the night, that stowed
Her in blue cobwebs of the moon.

Until a voice she hardly hears
Says turn your face,
Unlace the withered threads
That hold your smock,
Unbutton bolts of thawing ice,
Unlatch the crooked roots that green,
Your crown is pink —
Unfurling like a chestnut bud —
Now all is light and flash and flowing.

She lifts the gauze of dew
High in upstretched arms,
The sun unleashes her —
Spins her in its shaft.

The Last Dance

June is the cruellest month —
Before the monsoons come.

The jungle ticking with dry heat,
Weaver birds stitching their hanging nests.

Peacocks come early to the waterhole —
Clash for territory in flashy cock-fights,
Raise their tails in rattling fan-dance.

According to folklore
The hens are fertilized
By drinking tears
From the peacock's face.

Hypnotized by all the jewelled
Eyes, they covet the sapphires and emeralds,
To brighten their dowdy breasts,

Preferring the male
With the biggest tail —
Their god of war — destroyer of snakes.

From the highest trees
The smell of rain
Spices the wind.

The peacock is ready
He swoops down

The weight of his tail
Is lifted in stages —
It screens the clouds
That drift from the darkening horizon.

And whilst he forgets the tiger
Who wants revenge —
Coquettishly dances
The rhythm of rain —

The tiger has caught him
And feasts from a gem-strewn table.

Before the Lights Went Out

Emilia talks of her last hours with Desdemona

It was an ordinary Cyprus night —
Deep sky, cluttered with stars,
He had returned from the war
Hungry — drugged by the sight of her.

It was a marriage of minds, she said.
No one believed it to hear him talk —
There was a strangeness in the air,
My husband, for instance, obsessed with
                                    handkerchiefs.

When she started singing about the willow
I told her sad songs were not good for the child.
Later, when I saw that blood on the sheets
I knew he was killing two lives.

Before the lights went out
I remember the wind came up with such
An eerie whistling, I knew
There would be wrecking on the shore.

Entering Myth

Calypso, with arms outstretched,
Calls back her Ulysses.

Her body sends him out,
But all her island
Calls him back.

Each flipped sea bird's wing,
Every slender, dancing limb
Of sand-washed trees
Sings him home.

Calypso's arms are laden with longing,
Pearlised in the sun.
Her voice is anchored deep
Within her bedrock.

Half-hidden by the mast,
A sail between them now,
His wave a mere salute,
Ulysses turns his raft for Ithaca.

Now she's the one at sea,
Cross-currents pulling deeper,
Her emptiness opening

Like a vast cave
With wall paintings,
Untouched treasures,
Relics of mortals —
Space for so much imagining.

Horses

The cold penetrated their hooves until
Solid as Stonehenge they stood
Clamped to the land;

Breathed out long rasps of air
Which moved in misty folds around
Their magic ring.

The land beneath the snow lay blunt as iron,
Its memories of pasture
Locked inside.

Deep in the hoof of memory,
If memory they have,
The horses return to a new-blown sky,

Their manes splashed at the wind,
Whipped into skeins of silken thread,
That whispers like the slip of surf on stone.

Then further back to hot-coal heat of August,
The nodding fly-swarmed fields
Of downy weed —

Their sudden heavy gallop that echoed
Through the tinder earth with memories
Of ancient times —

The stamping ground of Pegasus,
High summits of Helicon where fountains
Gushed their succour.

The worldly wind brings music from far places,
Fragmented sounds diffuse the snowy silence,
The horses, notes, that petrify the song.

A Way of Looking

Once I'd seen them that way
It was hard to imagine ordinary lives
In overcrowded tenements.
— Precarious pillars of light —
Ephemeral in the haze across the bay.
We had to wait for evening to see them best;
They emerged from the rosy sky like
Athenian columns, decadent, not of this world.

But when we went up close
And saw the washing flap
From every flaking balcony
And not a Grecian god in sight
I wanted motes to cloud my eyes.

I'll always see them both ways
But know the frail ephemeral image
Is like imagination in the distance
That sometimes seems remote
And out of grasp.
But only waits for light to change
And then emerges slowly into focus,
Or in a flash is sudden and serene.

Acknowledgements

Acknowledgements are due to the editors of the following publications where some of these poems first appeared: *Outposts, Poetry Wales, The New Welsh Review, Envoi, Poetry Nottingham, Staple, Tees-Valley Writer, Bound Spiral.*

'Vanity', 'Change of Weather at Conwy', 'The Walled Orchard' and 'A Way of Looking' appeared in *Burning the Bracken: Fifteen Years of Seren Poetry* (Seren, 1996). 'Vanity' was in *Envoi Summer Anthology, 1991.* 'Return Fair Eve' appeared in *Windfall* (Kettleshill Press). 'Siesta' was in *Poems '92 Lancaster Literature Festival Competition Anthology.* 'Prinsengracht 263-Amsterdam' and 'Letter to Rodin' were in *Poems from the Readaround: Manchester Poets, 1995* (Tarantula Press).

Thanks are also due to BBC Radio Network North West, who have broadcast some of the poems on 'Write Now'.

'No Blossoms in Dubrovnik' was a prize-winner in the Southport Open Poetry Competiton, 1993. 'At Lidice' was a prize-winner in the International World View Poetry Competition, 1996.